Shoes

BEFORE THE STORE

BY RYAN JACOBSON · ILLUSTRATED BY DAN McGEEHAN

Published by The Child's World®
1980 Lookout Drive • Mankato, MN 56003-1705
800-599-READ • www.childsworld.com

ACKNOWLEDGMENTS
   The Child's World®: Mary Berendes, Publishing Director
   The Design Lab: Design and production
   Red Line Editorial: Editorial direction
   Content Consultant: S. Jack Hu, Ph.D., J. Reid and Polly Anderson Professor of Manufacturing
   Technology, Professor of Mechanical Engineering and Industrial and Operations Engineering,
   The University of Michigan

ISBN 9781609736811
LCCN 2011940077

PHOTO CREDITS
Igor Goncharenko/Dreamstime, cover, 1, back cover; 1997 PhotoDisc, Inc., cover (inset), 1 (inset);
Bigstock, 5; Li Ding/iStockphoto, 7; Simply Creative Photography/iStockphoto, 9; Lothar Radscheid/
iStockphoto, 10, 30 (top); Olaf Speier/Bigstock, 17, 19, 25, 27, 30 (bottom), 31 (left); Roman Milert/
Bigstock, 23; Shutterstock Images, 26; Radu Razvan Gheorghe/Dreamstime, 29, 31 (right)

Design elements: Igor Goncharenko/Dreamstime

Printed in the United States of America

ABOUT THE AUTHOR

Ryan Jacobson is the author of nearly 20 books, including picture books, chapter books,
graphic novels, choose-your-path books, and ghost stories. He lives in Mora, Minnesota, with
his wife Lora, sons Jonah and Lucas, and dog Boo.

Contents

CHAPTER ONE

We All Use Shoes

We wear shoes every day. And we have different shoes for different reasons. We play in our tennis shoes. We put on dress shoes for holidays. We bring sandals to the beach. And we wear boots to play in the snow. Some people even rent shoes for weddings! We want our shoes to feel comfortable. They keep our feet safe from sharp things like glass. And they keep our toes warm. We want our shoes to look nice, too. Do you have a favorite pair of shoes? What kind are they? What do they look like?

There are many styles of shoes to wear.

All shoes have the same basic parts. The top is the upper. It covers your foot and wraps around the sides. Your foot goes beneath the upper. It rests on the **insole**. There is also a **sole**. The sole is the very bottom of the shoe. It is the part of the shoe that leaves footprints. Many shoes have laces or strings to tie together. If they do, they also have a tongue. This is the flap at the top.

Have you thought about how shoes are made? There are many steps. Shoes are made from many things. Some shoes might have rubber, cloth, plastic,

and even wood. Many shoes also use leather. This is made out of animal skin. The most common skin used is from a cow.

Shoes are made from many parts.

CHAPTER TWO

Making Leather

From a ranch, cows are sent to a place where they are **butchered**. Workers cut up a cow's meat. Its skin is also cut away. The skin is sent to a **tannery**. This is a factory where leather is made. Workers treat the skin with special **chemicals**. They make the hair fall off the skin. Then workers put the

Cow skins are not the only skins that become leather. Leather is also made from pigs, goats, sheep, alligators, snakes, and other animals.

Leather is often made from cow skin.

skin in a kind of salt. This turns the skin into leather. Workers dye the leather brown. They also add more chemicals to the leather. This makes it stronger. Then the leather is shipped to the shoe factory.

Cow skin becomes leather at a tannery.

CHAPTER THREE

At the Shoe Factory

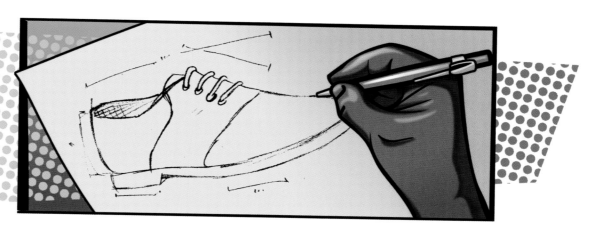

For many people, the way a shoe looks is just as important as how it fits. That is why shoes are designed by artists. These artists sketch ideas for

An artist sketches the shoes.

how the shoes will look. This is a design. They might draw dozens of different ideas before a design is chosen!

The final design it is sent to the Clicking Department. The design is drawn again. This time it is drawn on a **mold** shaped like a foot. It shows workers what the finished shoe will look like. People's feet are different sizes. So shoes need to be designed in different sizes, too. For this reason, the mold can be stretched apart and pushed together. It is used to design different sizes of shoes.

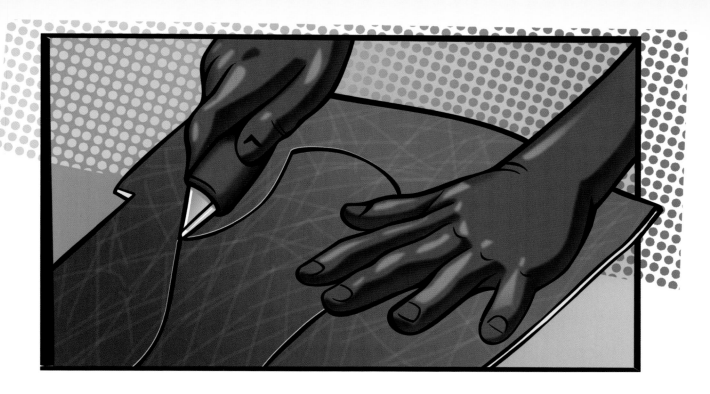

Workers first make the top of each shoe. This is the upper. A clicking operative does this step. This worker uses a pattern to cut leather by hand.

A worker cuts the leather.

After the pieces are cut, workers send them through a splitting machine. This machine shaves off a layer from the leather. All of the pieces of the leather are now the same thickness. Next, workers use a skiving machine. It cuts the leather's edges. It becomes thin. The thin edges are easier to sew together.

Leather has a natural pattern to it. Pieces for the left and right shoe need to look the same. The clicking operative cuts leather so that the natural designs are the same but opposite one another. If a clicking operative makes a mistake, the left and right shoes will not match!

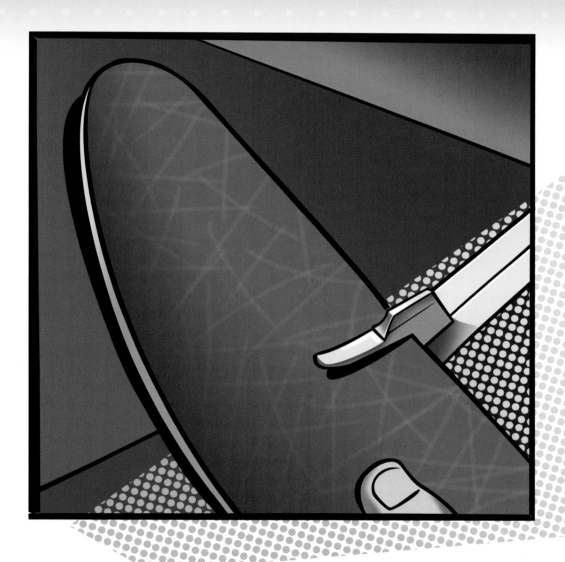

A skiving machine thins the leather.

The leather next goes to the Closing Department. The pieces of the upper are ready to be put together. The first pieces are sewn on a flat machine. The upper becomes curved and does not lie flat. It starts to look like a shoe. Workers now switch to a post machine. They finish sewing the upper.

Another worker hammers the stitches to smooth them and to flatten them. Then a worker glues leather strips around the upper's edges. The strips cover the upper's open sides. Last, the **eyelets** are added. These are the holes for shoelaces.

A worker sews the leather pieces together.

CHAPTER FOUR

Getting into Shape

Next, it is the Lasting Department's turn. Workers put a soft lining inside the uppers. Each upper goes around a plastic mold in the shape of a foot. It is called a **last**. The last keeps the upper in the shape of a shoe while the bottom is put together.

The bottom begins with an insole. The insole is glued to the upper's lining.

The shoes are put onto molds.

Workers put the shoe in another machine. It pulls the leather to make it straight. It takes out the wrinkles, too. The machine wraps the edges of the upper beneath the insole. Then it glues the pieces there. A worker grinds the bottom of the shoe on a machine until it is flat. Then the entire bottom part is coated with glue.

The shoe must be completely put together around the last. This makes the shoe have the right shape. But after the shoe is finished, the last is stuck inside. To remove the last, workers take off the insole. They take out the last. Then they glue the insole back into place.

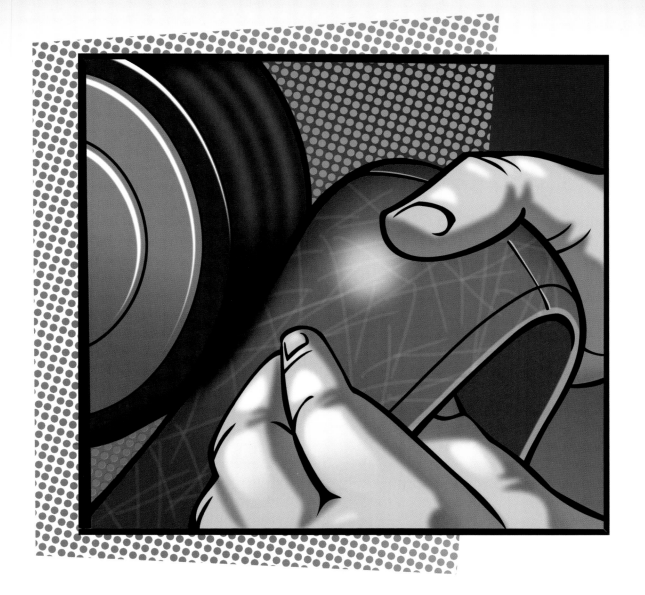

The bottom of the shoe is ground on a machine.

Workers make the sole of the shoe from leather, plastic, rubber, or wood. They shape it with cutting tools or a mold. Workers pour hot liquid material into a mold. The mold is a hollow container that is the shape of the sole. When the liquid cools, it becomes hard. Then it is taken out of the mold.

Workers press the sole onto the glue at the bottom of the shoe. After about ten minutes, the glue dries. It holds the sole in place. The shoes are now put together.

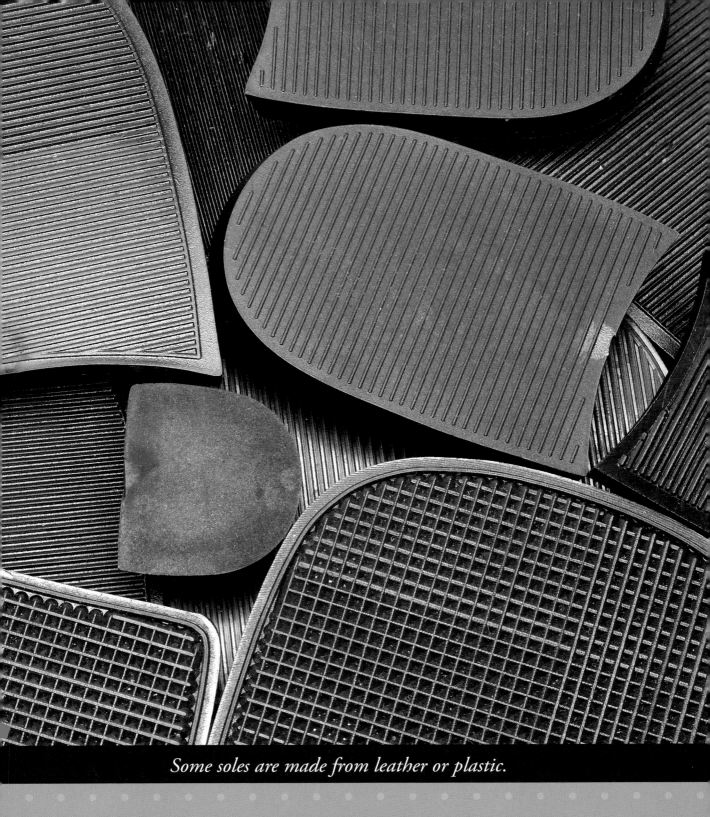

Some soles are made from leather or plastic.

CHAPTER FIVE

Good Looks

The shoes are not done yet, though. Their next stop is the Finishing Department. Workers trim the soles to make them smooth and even. They apply **stain** to color the shoes. They polish the shoes. This makes the shoes look clean and new. The shoelaces are laced in the eyelets. Then workers glue tags and labels inside the shoes.

The finished shoes are tested. Some tests are done by people. Other tests are done by machines.

Shoes are stained and polished.

The tests make sure the shoes have been made the right way.

Next, each pair of shoes is put into a box. They are bundled with other boxes and wrapped in plastic for shipping. Now they can be loaded onto trucks and shipped to shoe stores.

Laces go through the eyelets.

The average adult woman owns 17 pairs of shoes!

A worker puts shoes into boxes.

CHAPTER SIX

Onto Your Feet

Shoes arrive at sports stores, department stores, and shoe stores. Some stores put all the boxes out. They set them together by style and size. Other stores put out just one pair. Then a store worker finds your size and helps you try on the shoes. People can also buy shoes on the Internet. They find their size and the style they like. Then the shoes are sent right to their homes.

What kind of shoes do you like best? Are blue flats or red sneakers your style? You can pick shoes with

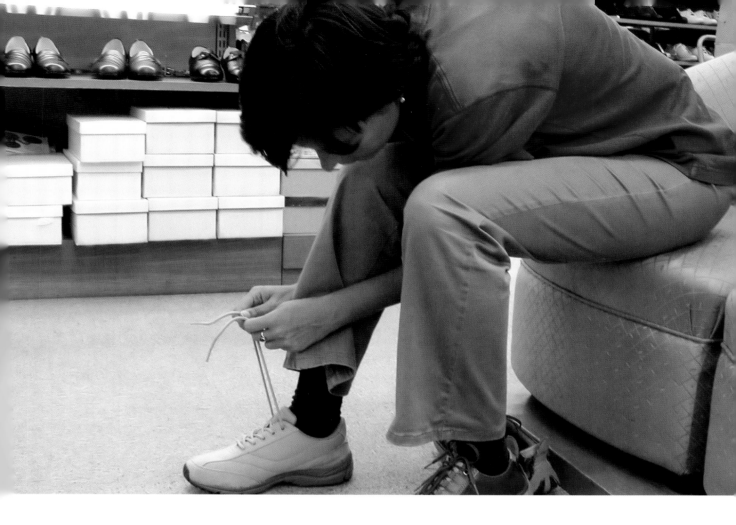

stripes or checker designs on them, too. Be sure to try them on, though. You want them to feel just right. They should not be too tight or too loose. Did you find the right fit? Good! Enjoy your new shoes!

People try on shoes to see if they fit.

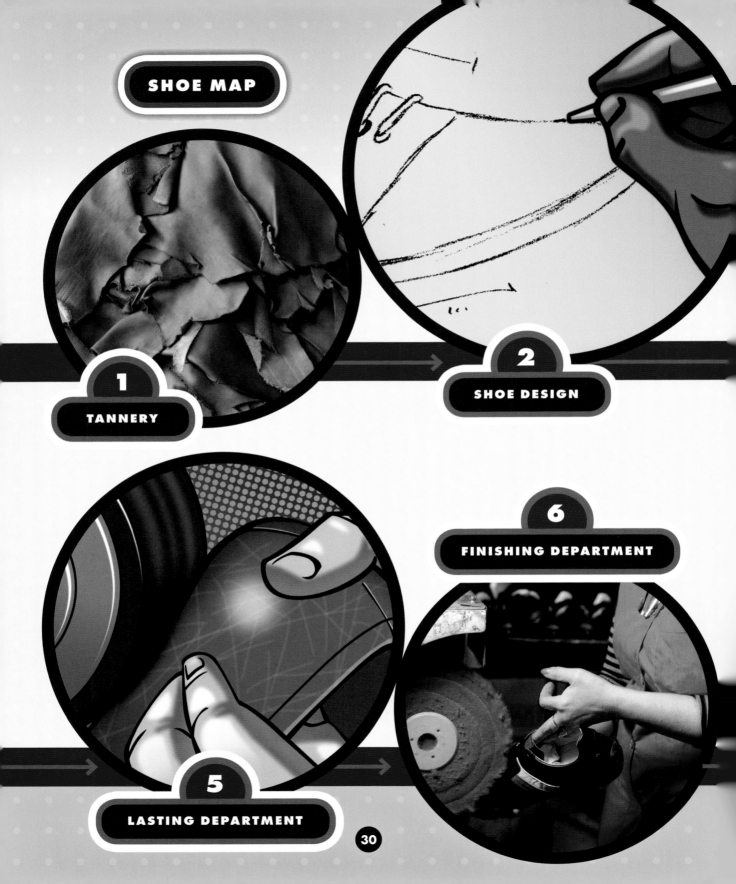

SHOE MAP

1 TANNERY

2 SHOE DESIGN

6 FINISHING DEPARTMENT

5 LASTING DEPARTMENT

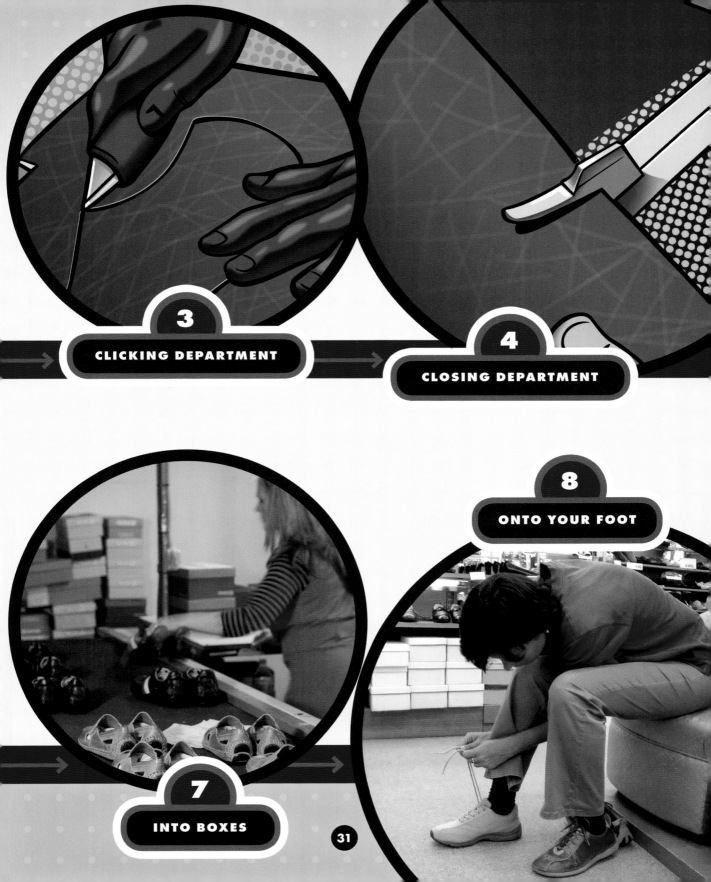

3
CLICKING DEPARTMENT

4
CLOSING DEPARTMENT

8
ONTO YOUR FOOT

7
INTO BOXES

31

GLOSSARY

butchered (BUCH-urd): A butchered cow has been cut up for its meat to be sold. A cow's skin is made into leather after it is butchered.

chemicals (KEM-uh-kuhlz): Chemicals are substances made using chemistry. Chemicals are used to treat cow skin.

eyelets (EYE-letz): Eyelets are small round holes in leather that are used to thread laces through. Shoelaces go through a shoe's eyelets.

insole (IN-sole): An insole is the part inside a shoe that your foot rests upon. An insole sits inside a shoe.

last (LAST): A last is a piece of hard plastic that is shaped like a foot. Shoes are made on a last.

mold (MOHLD): A mold is a hollow container that you put something into to set its shape or a solid piece used to hold the shape of something. Some soles are made using a mold.

sole (SOLE): A sole is the bottom part of a shoe. The sole is what makes a shoe print on the ground.

stain (STAYN): A stain is a dye that is used to color leather or wood. A brown stain is put on some shoes.

tannery (TAN-ner-ee): A tannery is a place where animal skin is made into leather. The tannery sends leather to a shoe factory.

BOOKS

MacDonald, Fiona. *Shoes and Boots Through History*. New York: Gareth Stevens Publishing, 2006.

Meachen Rau, Dana. *Athletic Shoes*. Ann Arbor, MI: Cherry Lake Publishing, 2007.

Swinburne, Stephen R. *Whose Shoes? A Shoe for Every Job*. Honesdale, PA: Boyds Mills Press, 2010.

INDEX

Visit our Web site for links about shoe production: childsworld.com/links

Note to Parents, Teachers, and Librarians: We routinely verify our Web links to make sure they are safe and active sites. So encourage your readers to check them out!